Counted Out

A Look Inside One Sergeant's Physical, Mental, and Spiritual War

Author

Corwyn Collier

Collier Elite Publishing

Stow, Ohio

Printed in the United States of America

Book Cover designed by Miguel Hernandez of Studio JS

Author photograph by Natasha Herbert

Edited by Eryka Parker of Lyrical Innovations, LLC

ISBN: 978-1-7379302-0-4

First Edition: 2021

10 9 8 7 6 5 4 3 2

Contents

DEDICATION

For my wife, Iisha Collier, my rock whose drive and constant love has helped me to accomplish more than anyone believed I could.

For my children (Malachi, Corwyn, and Aaron). You boys are my why.

For my father Felton Collier, I can never repay you for everything, but I promise to keep making you proud.

For my mother Vickie Collier, Thank you for the countless conversations and love over these last few years.

For my brother and sister, Felton and Victoria, I thank you both for being there during one of the most difficult times in my life and continuing to be there.

FOREWORD

In 2005, I had the pleasure of meeting Corwyn "CJ" Collier while we both worked at the Finish Line shoe store at Chapel Hill Mall. I was drawn to CJ because of his determination and excitement to get to know me. Shortly after going out on a couple of dates, CJ told me he was going to join the military to have a better opportunity to live his life and to fight for our country. At first I was upset that the person I had fallen in love with was leaving but I knew it was not goodbye.

While CJ was away, we wrote lots of letters back and forth and decided to move in together. Upon picking him up from basic training and his AIT training and graduation in July of 2006, I knew we would eventually get married. CJ proposed to me on December 10, 2006. I knew then that our love would stand the test of time due to the way we worked together as a team, the way we communicated, and the level of respect that we both had for each other.

When CJ finally did deploy to Iraq, we had a small wedding, just in case something did happen to him while overseas. This would allow my family to be protected and have access to him if he was ever injured. It was a blessing for us to have my grandparents as well as our parents telling us to have our wedding sooner and have a larger wedding later because we weren't able to see the storm ahead of us.

I will never forget the day that I received the call that CJ was injured. I was taking a nap at my mother's house because I'd just taken Benadryl for a bad case of allergies. I received a phone call from a strange number and since CJ was overseas, I answered my phone no matter what. I remember walking out of my mother's house to the end of the driveway to hear better. The Red Cross explained that CJ was badly injured and they did not know the status of his injuries or if he would survive. I was told that I would have to fly to Landstuhl, Germany to see him. I dropped to my knees and my mother, who'd been watching, instantly knew that something had happened to CJ.

I've had the pleasure of knowing Sergeant Corwyn "CJ" Collier, Sr., for 16 years. We've been married for 13 years and have three sons together, Malachi, Corwyn, and Aaron. Sgt. Collier has always given his purest heart to anything that he's valued. He's a man that loves God, is a committed husband, a dedicated father, and a devoted track coach to his athletes. Sgt. Collier exuberates honor and integrity in everything that he does. We've always lived by two quotes "It's not about the disability, it's about the ability" and "You never lose, you either win or you learn" by Nelson Mandela.

Counted Out: A Look Inside One Sergeant's Physical, Mental and Emotional War is a thought-provoking, spiritual journey of fighting for what everyone told you that you couldn't have or what you couldn't obtain. Counted Out puts on display the magnitude, grit, and perseverance that's needed to fight a physical, mental and emotional battle within oneself.

Sgt. Collier gracefully displays his commitment to himself and his family by not giving up through challenging times, times of despair, and times when his doctors Counted him Out.

Iisha Collier, wife of Sgt. Corwyn "CJ" Collier

ONE

We all have specific dates in our lives that hold significance for us. Be it a special anniversary, the birth of a child, your college graduation date, or the day you decided to get sober, these sentimental moments help shape who we are and leave lasting imprints on our lives. Not all memories associated with these dates are pleasant. Some dates may have mental or emotional scarring associated with them. Those painful moments are just as important as the joyous ones we celebrate. Some, however, can change the scope of your life forever. One of the most memorable and pivotal days for me was May 23, 2009. Before I go into detail about that day, let me first explain the events leading up to it.

Just like everyone else, I've always had dreams and goals that I wanted to accomplish in my life. As a youth, I set goals of competing in the Olympics and being a professional athlete. I attended college on a track scholarship and was an All-American, All-Conference athlete with a list of other great achievements to boot. After sustaining a torn quad muscle injury in 2004, I realized that my Olympic dreams might never happen. After graduating from college in 2005, I joined the workforce. Although I was blessed to be employed, I never felt satisfied or happy with my roles. Most of the time, I felt unfulfilled.

After working for about nine months in the car rental and retail industries, I decided to join the Army National Guard to serve my country because I wanted to do something bigger than myself. After careful evaluation, I decided to join. I was inspired by my brother and an older cousin who had both served in the Marine Corps and were deployed to Iraq. So, on March 1, 2006, I signed my contract to serve as a military police officer in the army. By serving in this role, my aim was to earn a new skill set that would be useful as a civilian.

My Journey to Iraq

Two years after joining the military, I was engaged with two small sons and was working as a claims adjuster. It was also during this time that my National Guard unit received the news that we were being deployed to Iraq at the beginning of the following year. I wasn't too concerned about being deployed because both my brother and cousin had previously completed tours of duty in Iraq. Several friends of mine had also gone to Iraq, so I didn't think I had much to fear. We trained for the remaining months leading up to the deployment, preparing for every possible situation we could face. I felt confident that I was ready and just wanted to do my job and safely return home to my family.

Our time in Iraq was no different than that of most other soldiers. We did missions six days a week, constantly living life one day at a time against the constant unknown. I was the leader of the Bravo Team of War Dawg, 2nd squad, fourth platoon. Military police, or MPs, work in three-man teams that consist of a driver, a gunner, and a team leader. There are four teams in a squad. I was always second in our convoy whenever we went on patrols. On occasion, I would lead the convoy, which is significant in how this particular story develops.

I had no idea that May 23, 2009 would become a significant date for me because it began like any other day. We had our usual morning briefing, then prepared for patrols. In the military, you are used to things malfunctioning, so when two of our trucks went down that morning, it didn't seem like a big deal. We easily acquired replacement trucks and our mission continued as scheduled. But for this mission, my team served as the lead for the convoy since we were in one of the bigger vehicles.

The day seemed very normal. Nothing was out of the ordinary. After our checks at the police stations, we made our way back to base. As we headed toward the highway to exit the city, a loud explosion rocked our convoy. The blast rattled all four vehicles in the convoy, but the actual blast only struck my vehicle.

Initially, I had no idea what happened and was slightly dazed and confused for a few moments. Once I attempted to look around to figure out what had occurred, I realized a bomb had struck me. We soon discovered that my team and I'd been hit by a roadside bomb, better known to us as an explosively formed penetrator (EFP). Our vehicle was immobilized, and I was pinned inside my truck.

I looked to my right, where the bomb had detonated, and saw nothing but blood covering the door and window beside me. This was when I realized I'd actually been hit. When I pulled up my right hand from the safety of the door, it was completely mangled from the bomb. Due to the bravery of a contractor who was in the vehicle with us, I received immediate first aid care. He began bandaging my hand to stop the bleeding. As he worked on my hand, I began the difficult process of trying to free my leg that was wedged between my caved-in door and the dashboard. The process was exhausting, strenuous, and terrifying. No matter how hard I tried, I just couldn't free my leg. The longer I worked at it, the more hope surely but slowly faded away.

Little did I realize that my vehicle sat directly on top of the blast as the EFP had stopped right beneath my seat. The smoldering shrapnel from the blast burned the back of my legs, severing an artery in my right leg which resulted in massive blood loss. As I lay bleeding, I fought to remain calm. The entire time, all I could think about was how desperately I wanted to live and see my family again. I didn't want to die.

As I struggled to stay conscious, I reflected on the night before when I'd wished my two-year-old son a happy birthday. All I could think about was the birthday boy and my oldest son who was five-years-old at the time. The only thing that mattered to me at that moment was getting back home to be with my wife and my boys. So, I did the only thing that I knew I could be certain of that would help me get back to my family. I looked to God and prayed. I didn't care what type of physical shape I was in. All I cared about was making it back home to be with the ones I loved more than life itself. I asked Him for two simple things. *Please let me see my sons grow up and allow me to be with my wife.*

By God's grace, my squad arrived to evacuate me and the rest of my team from the remains of our vehicle. Once I snuck a peek down at my bloodied, mangled entanglement of muscle, skin, and bone that once was my fully functional leg, the surging adrenaline waned. Cue the excruciating pain. When it fully hit me, I screamed.

But when the metal had to cut through me all over again, all of that adrenaline shit went out the window. They laid me on a stretcher to transport me to the next available truck. It was at this moment that I did the one thing I had known better not to do; I looked down at my leg. The sight of all the blood and mangled flesh and bones was definitely a crazy sight. All I could think about was having my leg amputated and having to walk around like comedian Katt Williams' *Little Tink Tink* character with the aluminum legs on the racing track.

Once my team loaded me onto a truck, I was headed to meet a MedVAC to fly me to the hospital. I was joined by my good friend Sergeant Bartish, a.k.a. Scuba Steve, the nickname I gave him due to his resemblance to the character Adam Sandler played in "Big Daddy". Having Steve with me helped me get through the pain and trauma of what had just occurred. While his presence did wonders for my morale, the pain quickly grew intolerable. To help manage the pain, the medics planned to give me a morphine injection once they stabilized my leg. As they bandaged my leg to stop the bleeding and limit the risk of infections, I asked Steve to promise me something. If anything happened to me, I wanted him to look out for my sons. He reassured me that I was going to make it back home to look out for them myself, but I needed to know that someone I knew and trusted would be there for my sons, just in case. Knowing the kind of man Steve was gave me great comfort. There was never a doubt that he would keep his promise and look after my boys.

To my surprise, the medic looked to Scuba Steve and said, "I want you to grab his pants real tight and inject the morphine in the side of his hip."

Steve replied, "Okay, I got it. No problem."

It's still unclear to me, to this very day, if the driver hit a bump or if we swerved, but somehow, Scuba Steve managed to inject himself with *my damn morphine shot!* The frustrated medic sprang into action and administered the injection, which, in retrospect, is what he should have done in the first place. Meanwhile, Steve was high as a freakin' kite and in need of medical attention himself. As I reflect on that horrible, life-altering experience, I can't help but to be thankful of the straight comedy that ensued, which was exactly what the doctor ordered.

As we arrived at the landing zone, the medical helicopter was waiting there for me. My squad surrounded me one last time before they loaded me onto the Blackhawk. I appreciated the way they comforted me with encouraging words that I'll always remember and cherish. On our flight to the hospital, the medics talked to me, doing their best to try to keep me calm. I vividly remember talking to them about Lebron James and the Cavs, as I'm a huge fan. Since it was late May, the NBA playoffs were in full swing. Despite my serious injuries, I had to know how my team was doing.

When we finally landed at the Combat Support Hospital (CSH), we were met by a team of nurses and doctors who rushed me inside. After playing 50 questions, which wasn't so bad, I did my best to keep myself in good spirits by acting like a straight up clown. Even in the face of death, my personality didn't change. For example, the nurse asked my name and I replied, "They call me Big Sexy, but for medical purposes, you can call me Sergeant Collier." I remember how we both laughed, which was the best self-therapy I could have given myself. The foolishness continued once they began cutting off my uniform to attend to my injuries.

"WAIT!" I yelled out. Everyone froze and I began to pat my crotch. I sighed dramatically with relief upon confirming that my manhood was still in place. Amidst the measured chuckles in the room, I overheard one of the nurses saying, "Why is this every man's concern when they come in here?" *Did she really have to ask?*

A Miracle and Rebirth

Now, this was where things got a little fuzzy for me. Shortly after being evacuated and treated at the hospital, my condition took a serious turn for the worst. Due to the massive amount of blood loss I experienced, I went into cardiac arrest. Just that quickly, I went from joking around with the hospital staff in good spirits to flatlining and banging on death's door. The Red Cross called my wife to inform her that my chances of survival weren't very good and that she would have to fly to Germany to see me for the last time. My wife recalls receiving that phone call as being one of the most difficult moments of her life. She was overwhelmed with fear and sadness. On top of that, she had to manage the concerns she had about our boys along with the other tremendous responsibilities that awaited her. In my absence, she was left alone to figure out how to explain everything to our young kids.

Even though I was a soldier on the other side of the world fighting a war, it was my wife who got on her knees and fought the good fight through her prayers. As she prayed for me back home, I did my best to fight for my own life. The doctors used a defibrillator on me three times to get my heart beating again. However, there was not enough blood banked at the facility to replace all the blood I lost. To help stabilize me, the medical staff rallied thirteen soldiers to donate blood on-site.

After receiving the blood transfusion, the Red Cross called my wife back to let her know that I had been stabilized and I was going to make it. She would be able to visit me in Washington D.C. at the Walter Reed Army Medical Center.

It was official. On May 23, 2009, I survived what would later be known as my Alive Day. If you're unfamiliar with this term, Alive Day is the date of a very close brush with death. For me, it's the date I was severely injured, which thankfully happens to correspond with the day I was born again and received a second chance at life.

TWO

Two days later, I woke up in Germany. I remember being disoriented, but thankful to be alive. To my surprise, my right leg was still connected to my body. However, I wasn't thrilled to have a breathing tube down my throat, which was the most uncomfortable thing I'd ever experienced. It wasn't long after waking up that I made an attempt to pull the damn tube out. My nurse rushed into the room and started yelling, "No, no! Stop!" Eventually, the doctor came in and safely removed the tube for me, which enabled me to talk.

The first thing I did was request a call home to speak with my wife, who I assumed had to be worried to death about me. However, my initial call home did not go as you may be expecting. After my initial greeting to my wife, I'd asked, "How are my Cavs doing in the playoffs?" I could only imagine the look of confusion on her face.

She completely ignored my question and replied, "Somebody called and said you'd been hurt and almost lost your life and now you're asking about the Cavs? What's going on?"

I responded, "Yeah, I got hit by a bomb. But, for the most part, I'm good. They stabilized me and saved my leg, looks like. They're flying me to D.C."

"Are you sure you're okay?" Iisha asked.

"I'm good, but you still ain't let me know about the Cavs."

"Boy, I ain't thinkin' 'bout no Cavs. I'll see you in D.C."

If you have never been transported in a hospital bed over the Atlantic Ocean on a military plane, trust me, that shit was **terrible**! I was in pain for the duration of the nine-hour flight. If that wasn't enough, my gurney repeatedly rammed into the side of the plane. My nurse was no help at all; she was too busy enjoying her iPod and magazines to pay me much attention or attend to my needs. When we finally landed in D.C., I breathed a sigh of relief, as I was one step closer to being with my family.

A New Life - Walter Reed Army Medical Center

Upon my arrival in D.C., I was transported to Walter Reed Army Medical Center and placed in the ICU, where I remained until I was stable enough to be placed in a ward. As soon as I reached my room, I was thrilled to see my family there to greet me. My father, brother, sister, sister-in-law, and wife were all there with smiles and tears. The love they displayed was beyond the magnitude of anything I had ever felt before.

I was eventually moved to Ward 59, a place where life changed for me. It was there that I suffered constant nightmares about the event that almost took my life. Most of the dreams were so vivid and real that I often woke up screaming out for members of my military unit. Each time, the nurses rushed into my room to calm me down. The recurring nightmares had eventually invaded dreams about my civilian life. For instance, I once dreamt of walking down the road back at home, while texting on my Sidekick. The next thing

I knew, the phone exploded in my hand, blowing me backward. The nightmares went on for months during my hospital stay. Getting a good night's sleep was difficult at times and the medication they gave me didn't always help. During the nights I couldn't sleep, I watched plenty of episodes of Spongebob and Harry Potter.

When I wasn't preoccupied with battling insomnia and nightmares, I was on the operating table. It felt like every time I turned around, someone was cutting on me. The only good thing about the countless surgeries that I endured was that being under general anesthesia might have been the only good sleep I got during my hospital stay.

Most of the surgeries I had were aimed at recovering the use of my hand and leg. After surgery, I underwent physical therapy multiple days per week. Due to my hand injury in the explosion, rehabilitating my right hand was the most interesting process I've experienced. In order to regain functionality in my hand, the doctors had to first reattach it to my body. This allowed for the regeneration of the nerves in my hand. They also used the excess skin from my side to replace the skin on my hand. The procedure included cutting my right side open and directly attaching my hand to it. For five weeks, I looked like a little teapot and couldn't even move my hand at all. Talk about being uncomfortable. Whenever I had a random itch on the left side of my body, I had no way to scratch it. Do you know how humiliating it is to have to call for a nurse just to help you scratch an itch you can't reach? Humbling but embarrassing too. Here I am this grown man who can't even scratch his shoulder because I looked like a little teapot.

The injuries to my right leg were extensive. The shrapnel from the blast essentially shredded the muscle and bones in my lower leg. My leg was damaged to the point where the surgeons at Walter Reed had to remove my fibula, the smaller of the two bones in my lower leg, along with half of my calf muscle. Even though the fibula is the smaller of the two bones, surgeons had to ensure that the major weight-bearing bone in the leg was strong enough to support my weight. During my rehab, I remained in an external halo for six months to allow my leg to heal. During that time, I needed a few more surgeries to fix my shattered leg. The fact that my leg did not require amputation is living proof that God is in the miracle-making business.

One day, while my wife and I were in the room after a day of X-rays and CT scans, my doctor came in and dropped a heavy bomb on us. He informed us that I had blood clots in my lungs and my leg. This was some scary news on top of all the other issues I was already dealing with at that time. My doctor prescribed Lovenox, an anticoagulant or blood thinner, to prevent blood clots and reassured me the medication would significantly reduce my risk for developing future blood clots.

After my bout with blood clots, depression began to settle in. Even with my wife and family there with me, I still found myself slipping into a dark place. On most days, I didn't want to eat or leave my room. I just felt alone. I remember wanting to die early on in my recovery. I had given up and felt that my quality of life would not be what I wanted it to be. I didn't want to be a burden to my family and felt it would be easier for everyone, especially me if I was no longer around. As I sank further into a depressive state, I found myself feeling as if God had let me down. I no longer cared about practicing my religion and didn't have much use for praying at that point because I felt as though God wasn't listening. Whenever my dad prayed over me, I complied out of respect for him. As I lay there feeling sorry for myself, I couldn't bring myself to understand how this had happened to me. In my mind, I'd lived a good life and considered myself to be a faithful, upright man of God. I believed I'd done things the right way and lived a pious Christian life. I didn't deserve to be struck down like that. In the blink of an eye, my gift for running track was taken from me and life as I knew it would never be the same.

On my worst days, I openly welcomed death. Somehow, God's gentle voice and His divine presence kept me grounded in my faith and always led me back to continuing the good fight. I had two sons that I'd asked God to ensure that I was around to raise. I had to find peace with what had occurred and figure out my next steps. Anger and resentment weren't going to help me rid myself of depression. I knew I had to figure out a plan, and soon.

My fight to recover began with physical therapy. As I previously mentioned, the multiple surgeries that I endured required me to learn how to walk and stand on my own legs again after months of being bedridden. It was a moment I had been waiting on and I knew it would be an opportunity for me to push past part of my depression. All I needed was the ability to simply stand up and move on my own two legs. The nurses transported me down to the therapy room and my doctor positioned me up on the balance beams. It was there that God made His down payment on the miracle that changed my life. It was at that moment that I took my first steps on the long road to recovery and more importantly, discovery. In my mind, I was a twenty-seven-year-old soldier who had been walking for at least twenty-six of those years. Admittedly, there was a tinge of arrogance sweeping through my mind, as I figured taking those first steps would be a walk in the park, pun intended.

"On the count of three, we are going to stand up," the doctor told me. "One, two, three! Up!"

It was at that moment that I fully realized just how difficult the rehabilitation process was going to be. I just wasn't ready; physically or mentally. I couldn't believe that something as simple as putting one foot in front of the other - a process I took for granted every day of my life - was suddenly something I'd have to work at mastering all over again.

I sat back down after feeling unbearable pain in my leg. The initial setback humbled me. I didn't have long to feel sorry for myself before the doctor began encouraging me to give it another go. The competitor in me would not allow me to accept defeat. I had to give it another try. My doctor told me that the goal was for me to be able to stand on my own for at least ten seconds. On the count of three, I braced myself to stand up again.

Again, I failed, as I was unable to endure the pain in my right leg. I couldn't believe how a task as simple as standing could be so difficult. I felt defeated and heartbroken. I was ready to give up. I'd never thought that something I'd been able to do my entire life would become such a difficult task.

To her credit, my doctor encouraged me to give it one more try; but this time, for only five seconds. The shorter timeframe made the goal seem more attainable, which made me all the more determined to reach it. *Five seconds shouldn't be too difficult,* I thought. I attempted to stand for the third time, only to fail once again. It was the last failure that caused me to burst into tears. Not man tears, but full-out toddler tears accompanied by snot bubbles and drool.

Having my wife and oldest son by my side during physical

therapy made dealing with my failure to walk more bearable. When I wanted to give up—which seemed like every other day—they kept me encouraged and motivated. It didn't matter how small or insignificant I felt the progress I made was; they continued to cheer me on, which was sorely needed.

Despite my family's continued encouragement and support, there were still days that I could not shake free of the feeling that I was failing at getting back to myself. As I reflect back on those long days and lonely nights of lying in bed, recovering from various surgeries, I remember how much I longed to get back on my feet and walk again. I never imagined that learning to walk again would be so difficult. It was a battle that I was losing badly. Not only was I losing the battle, but it seemed that I was also destined to lose the war to reclaim my life.

Without my wife's unwavering support, there's no way I would have made it through those grueling physical therapy sessions. But what I'm most grateful to her for is the way she refused to allow me to remain in a place of self-pity. I remember leaving physical therapy one day in a wheelchair with my head down and eyes brimming with tears. I was feeling low that day. As I rolled back to my room, feeling sorry for myself, I felt a powerful slap across the back of my head. My wife was finally fed up with me. During those two long months, she had been putting up with me and my constant "woe is me" mentality. She stepped around the front of my chair and stopped me dead in my tracks. Then she bent down and said something to me I will never forget.

"You need to stop all this damn crying!" she said. "You need to man up and be the man you used to be. We knew this wasn't gonna be easy, but you are crying in front of your son who needs you. If you want your life back, take it back!"

Her words forced me to accept the fact that my recovery was going to be solely on me and that no one else was going to learn to walk for me. If I was ever going to walk again, I had to put in the work and make it happen. Not the doctors or my family. If I wanted to have a life worth fighting for, I had to accept the fact that pain would be a part of the journey. I needed to get in the proper mindset and be ready to endure the pain and discomfort that came with fighting to reclaim my life.

THREE

The long road to learning to walk again started out with learning how to get my reconstructed leg used to the pressure of supporting my weight while standing again. Each morning, after my usual check-in, which included bandaging, getting my temperature and blood pressure checked, etc., I sat myself up in bed and allowed my legs to dangle over the edge of the bed. This used to be very painful in the beginning and I would have to literally bite down on my pillow to brace myself for the pain. Thankfully, the routine became easier and less painful over time. As such, I needed a new challenge to keep me on track with my goal of walking out of that hospital on my own legs.

After a few days of hanging my legs, I devised a new plan. I put off physical therapy for about ten days to get myself mentally prepared to move forward with the new task of standing while slightly leaning back onto the bed for support. This was something I thought of on my own and without authorization from any of the medical staff. No one had a clue about what I was up to. The medical staff would never have approved of this exercise because I had no safety precautions in place to keep me from falling and re-injuring myself. It was my renewed determination to create a new life for myself that propelled me to take those risks. I was slowly changing. Not only was I rehabilitating my body, I was also strengthening and sharpening my soul.

I was in a different space mentally when I finally returned to PT. The doctors placed me back in the balance beams and stood me upright. From there, I boldly took my first step forward, and another, and another until I finally made it to the end of the balance beam, where a chair was waiting for me to rest. That moment meant everything to me. It was a moment of triumph, which I desperately needed to restore my confidence. I was finally able to walk again, although it was in beams. As I celebrated, I reflected on the tough love my wife had shown me. It was her refusal to allow me to wallow in my heart that propelled me to that victory. Aided by her strength and God's favor, I began turning the tide on winning the war to reclaim my life.

With a renewed sense of hope and determination, I continued to press on toward achieving my goal of walking again. As time went on, my PT regimen expanded to consist of learning how to safely transfer myself from my bed to my wheelchair and back. Soon, I learned how to safely stand in the shower. These were a few of the required tasks I needed to be able to perform on my own in order to be released to the Fisher House, a step-down facility where soldiers were able to complete physical and occupational therapy without being in a hospital. Being discharged to the Fisher House represented a major benchmark in my recovery, as it was considered the halfway point for me going back home.

Another breakthrough in my road to recovery occurred in mid-July when my frat brothers drove up to spend a few days with me in the hospital—having my brothers there to uplift me provided the boost I needed to embark upon my longest walk while in the hospital. It was a special moment I'll never forget. I asked them if they wanted to accompany me to my PT session, and of course, they agreed. With my frat brothers cheering me on, I was able to go farther than I'd ever gone before without requiring any breaks. I'll never forget how it felt to share that moment with people who were such a big part of my life.

With my unit set to return home from deployment, my sole focus was walking again when they landed. It was going to be a big surprise for them. I went from using a walker to walking with the assistance of crutches. Finally, I was able to comfortably walk using only a cane. Although I was still using a wheelchair to cover far distances, I was moving along at a great pace and was far removed from my initial post-injury status. Walking, thankfully, finally started to feel like second nature to me again.

Although my physical therapy and recovery were progressing well, mentally, things were not so great. Hospital life was beginning to feel more like being on lockdown. It felt as if I were trapped in a cage. I knew I needed to get out of there and fast. I was grateful and relieved when the hospital granted me a day pass to be with my family away from the facility. I spent the day shopping at the mall with my wife and we decided to catch a movie afterward.

I hadn't been officially diagnosed, but I learned on that afternoon that Post-Traumatic Stress Disorder (PTSD) is very real. After the incident, I'd spoken to a psychologist who asked me questions to determine my mental health status. During our conversations up until that point, he hadn't mentioned PTSD and I hadn't experienced any severe complications from it besides my recurring nightmares. Honestly, I didn't want to be associated with the stigma of PTSD because of all it entailed. But during our movie date that day, I definitely got a rude awakening of how apparent it was in my life. I wanted to see the new G.I. Joe movie because I'd read and enjoyed the novel on which the movie was based on while in the hospital. I was excited about seeing the movie because I was a big fan of the G.I. Joe cartoon as a child. My childhood memories were not enough to prepare me for the opening scene. I was not ready. At all.

In the opening scene of the movie, a convoy of soldiers were out on patrol. Sound familiar? I think you know what happens next. The convoy, of course, comes under attack by heavy artillery. I was still okay at that point, until an artillery shell hit a truck. Upon hearing Marlon Wayans' character scream out, "my leg is pinned," a flashback of my truck being attacked raced through my mind. Without warning, my heart began to pound against my chest. Struck with raw fear, all I could do was place my head down and pull my hood over my face. I took deep breaths to calm myself. My wife immediately noticed my reaction and leaned over to ask if I was okay. I immediately questioned whether or not I was fit to watch a movie like that without feeling like I was literally reliving the scariest moment of my entire life. I told myself, *It's just a movie, it's just a movie, it's just a movie.* Eventually, my heart rate slowed down, and I was somehow able to watch the rest of the movie with no further issues.

As odd as it may sound, I'm actually grateful for that situation. I kept telling myself that I was okay, but in reality, I wasn't. I learned that although I was on pace for physical recovery, I'd never really given my mental state much attention. That experience helped me realize how important prioritizing my mental health was for my holistic healing journey. I knew that if I wanted to improve myself wholly, I'd have to face what happened to me. The healing process would have to take on a mental, physical, and spiritual path.

The first step I took on my road to mental recovery was developing the ability to talk about the attack. Engaging in open and honest dialogue about it allowed me to reflect on my experience. The more I engaged in dialogue, I realized that through it all, I was much stronger than I'd given myself credit for. Of all the types of therapy I experienced at Walter Reed Hospital, talking to others about the attack proved to be the most effective in helping me heal holistically. The more people I shared my story with, the more compelled I felt to keep sharing. I shared my story with every commander, general, and a celebrity that came through my hospital room door. Each time I attended a therapy session, I walked away armed with a different perspective and reaction to what took place on that dreadful day in Iraq. As more people heard my story, I became known as the storyteller of the ward.

Of all the amazing and wonderful people I shared my story with, God was by far my most important audience. Being able to finally pray again without feeling angry represented a pivotal moment in my recovery. I quickly learned that I absolutely needed prayer and peace of mind to fight my way back to living a somewhat normal life. There's no doubt in my mind that my experiences in the hospital were God's way of testing my resolve, my courage, and most importantly, my faith. Through it all, I rediscovered an old, yet faithful truth that the Almighty God I serve does hear and answer prayers.

At the outset of my recovery, my wife and father remained at my side daily. When they came to visit, we watched movies and enjoyed time outside on nice days to get fresh air. I appreciated having them both there; their presence and the wonderful conversations and laughs we shared helped take my mind off the pressure of my recovery process. Having them there to listen to my stories and occasional complaining made all the difference in the world.

On the weekend of 4th of July, my wife's best friend drove the boys up from Akron, Ohio to D.C. I hadn't seen them in six months to the day. When they walked through the door, my eyes filled with tears. I cried, thinking about how God had answered my prayer, "I don't care what happens to me, Lord. I just want to see my sons grow up." As I looked at them and hugged them, I realized God was real and that He knew that my boys needed me. Having the privilege of that moment along with celebrating my first wedding anniversary in the hospital was significant to me. They made me realize how special our family bond was.

As much as I enjoyed my wife and father's company, there were two very special people who I missed dearly. There wasn't a day that passed that I didn't yearn to see my sons. Initially, my plan was to hold off on seeing them until I was further along in my recovery.

An Unknown Void is Filled

Bonding with my family was important to me for many reasons. One of the most important reasons was taking the opportunity to provide my children with something I didn't have while growing up: a two-parent household. My father raised my older brother, myself, and my younger sister on his own. My parents divorced when I was about four years old and my mother dealt with personal issues that kept her absent from our lives until I was sixteen. The absence of a mother opens a wound in your heart that never really heals. The emotional damage, especially if it's in the first six years of your life, can be detrimental. When she returned, I was overjoyed, forgetting my fear of abandonment and fully ready to forgive her and move on. For a while, it seemed like she'd changed and that I would possibly have a mother again, then she disappeared from my life again after a few months.

So you can imagine my confusion when as I lay groggy from the anesthesia in the post-surgery recovery room at Walter Reed, a nurse said to me, "Your mom called to check on you." When the nurse said the word "mother", my immediate thought was that I was either hallucinating or that she was referring to my wife. When I questioned her about it, she replied, "No, she said she was your mother, Vickie."

I knew that name like I knew my own, so hearing it triggered some intense emotions in me. But I kept asking myself, *how could she have found me in this hospital?* Hell, how did she even know I was in the military? I'd never listed her as an emergency contact because I didn't have her contact information. I hadn't seen or spoken to her in eleven years.

As it turns out, my Uncle Emmanuel was the one responsible for locating and contacting my mother. His reason was simple; as my mother, he thought she had the right to know that something that traumatic had happened to me. Since I'm very close to my uncle, there was no love lost. I understood and respected what he was trying to do and couldn't be mad at him for the decision he'd made on my behalf. When the anesthesia completely wore off, I was able to talk to my mother on the phone. Even after all the years that had passed without us speaking, I still knew her voice. This sense of happiness overcame me. I instantly put any ill feelings to the side and enjoyed the relief affiliated with talking to my mother once again. After a while, she asked if she could visit me. At the time, I was unsure of how I felt about her coming or how to respond to her request. I knew I needed to first speak with my wife and father to let them know my mother had contacted me and to see how they felt about her visiting.

Having that conversation with my wife and father wasn't easy. I was familiar with my father's feelings about my mother. There was no resentment on his part, but he did feel a need to protect me from the potential disappointment of restarting a relationship with her. My wife, on the other hand, knew very little about my mother, which made it tough for her to form any real opinions about her. Together, we decided to allow her to visit and I'm glad we did. It was a chapter of my life that needed to be closed so that a new one could begin.

During my mother's first visit, we spent a great deal of time catching up on each other's lives. We shared stories and laughed about the different events that had transpired over the years. Ironically, my mom had been searching for us as well. She ran across my college track pictures on the internet but wasn't one-hundred percent sure that it was me because I'd always gone by my nickname, CJ. That's a long story for another time. The longer we talked, the more I realized how great it felt to have my mother in my life again. Despite how terrible my injuries were, I was grateful that they created the opportunity for me to reconnect with my mother. Her presence there with me during such a difficult time showed her love for me, which was key in helping me to forgive her and to heal in a different way. That moment was necessary to assist in my recovery. It was the first taste of post-traumatic growth I'd experienced. This concept, also known as benefit finding, is associated with positive change as a result of adversity and other challenges in order to rise to a higher level of functioning. I essentially developed a new way of understanding the world and my place in it. My personal process of change had just begun. Little did I know, it was God's way of helping me mentally prepare for the long road ahead.

FOUR

The days began moving quickly, bringing me closer to starting therapy and a series of surgeries. I was grateful that my wife consistently showed up and remained by my side, all while continuously working on her first Master's degree. Yes, she has more than one Master's. I was so proud of the progress she'd made, despite all of the unexpected disruptions in our lives. So when she mentioned planning to take the summer off from her program to focus on my recovery, I told her, "Don't you dare quit! You keep going. I'm not going anywhere."

Iisha earned a Bachelors in Education and worked hard to get her first teaching job. Even as a long-term substitute, she showed up for her students in amazing ways. She was an exceptional teacher and my personal source of inspiration. One day, as she was working on a paper while sitting next to my hospital bed.

I looked over at her and said, "I know what I want to do with my life after this."

"And what might that be?" she asked.

"I want to be a teacher, just like you," I said. "God has given me a second chance at life and I want it to have a purpose. I see how you change kids' lives each day and I want to do the same."

Iisha looked over at me, smiled, and said, "Go for it, babe. But you do realize we're about to be poor."

As we both laughed, I said, "We've got this."

Not long after having this discussion with my wife, I received a visit from an Army career and transition advocate. During the initial visit, we spoke about my long-term career goals. The career and transition advocate seemed excited for me and advised me that the Army had a program called "Troops to Teachers". This program was designed to encourage and assist soldiers with transitioning into the teaching field. I did some research on the program and thought it was a good fit for me. Although it would be a while before I would be released from the hospital, I still wanted to make sure a plan was in place to create a career opportunity for myself upon leaving the hospital.

The Long Surgical Road Ahead

As mentioned previously, I've endured countless surgeries. Of all the procedures I've had at Walter Reed, there was one in particular that stood out for a number of reasons. When the time came for me to have a skin graft to replace the burned skin of my right hamstrings and calf, I knew the importance of the procedure. But I was unaware that the surgeons needed to take skin from another part of my body to graft to my leg.

When you hear the term "skin graft" for the first time in the hospital, someone with limited medical knowledge might think of some cool science-fiction movie where the skin has already been manufactured elsewhere. Well, as it turned out, my theory was completely wrong. The surgeons explained their plans of grafting skin from my quads using lasers. Once again, I was baffled by all the medical advancements and technology the surgeons and doctors had at their disposal.

Based on the information given to me by the medical staff, I made a rash assumption that the procedure would be a rather simple one. That was not the case at all. As soon as I woke up from surgery, my quads felt as if they were **on fire**. I looked down and saw that the bandages were streaked with dried blood as the doctors explained that my wounds would heal in a few days. As was the case during the majority of my hospital stay, there was a twist to this plot.

After some time had passed, the doctor came back in and said, "It looks like those bandages are ready to come off." He placed a bottle of saline and scissors next to my bed. "Alright, this is what you need to do."

What do you mean by what I *need to do?* I thought. *You're the doctor, right? This is about what you've got to do!*

"As you can see, the blood has dried to the gauze pretty well," he said as he gave instructions on how to remove the bandages. "So, you'll need to take this saline to moisten it so we can cut it and pull it off."

I held my silence, but the entire time I'm certain my facial expression said, *Are you serious right now? You want me to wet my legs up and cut it with these scissors and peel it off, all with one hand?*

The doctor must have read the puzzled look on my face, as he was kind enough to demonstrate the process by making the initial cuts on the gauze, which he carefully peeled away.

Simple enough, I thought as I took over and began peeling away more gauze. The initial snips I took at the bandages posed very little trouble for me because they were away from the skin graft area, which was where all the action was. While the doctor watched me cut away, he neglected to mention that the dried blood around the area of the graft behaved like glue, thereby causing the bandages to stick to my wound. Of course, this made removing the bandages as painful as peeling away my own skin. Let's just say I felt like I'd worked a nine to five shift by the time I removed all of the bandages from both legs.

Admittedly, I shed a few tears during the painful process. At the conclusion of my struggles, I emerged with a wet ass from hours of pouring saline on my legs. I'll say this process taught me the true value of my right thumb. It was already difficult enough adjusting to the loss of my fingers, but to be placed in a position where I had to grip and tear away at things took me right out of the frying pan and straight into the fire.

Once all of the bandages were off, I turned my attention to my wounds. Surprisingly, my leg looked in relatively good shape after having the skin laser-removed. My real interest, though, was how the skin graft on my calf and hamstrings looked. Unfortunately, it would be a while before I could assess the results, as the skin was yet to heal in those areas. Nevertheless, I was blown away by all the cutting-edge medical technology at the doctors' disposal.

At the conclusion of my skin graft procedure, the medical team officially proclaimed that my legs had officially gained their tiger stripes. I was initially told that they would heal and look like the skin grafts never took place. Well, after eleven years, it's still obvious that I had a skin graft. I'm not ungrateful. I'm aware that I'm beyond blessed and I'm at peace that the skin will never be as it once was.

Next, it was time to prepare for what would be one of my final procedures. My tibia was healing nicely, but there was a missing bone, so a piece that resembled PAC-MAN's open mouth was still in place to prevent my leg from snapping in the future. The doctors opted to avoid using metal rods and screws to avoid possible infection as it would then require an amputation. Yes, hearing the word amputation resulted in some scary thoughts for me.

Additionally, the surgeons informed me of their plans to do a bone graft, which consisted of shaving off some of my femur bone to replace the bone missing in my tibia. Of course, I went along with the procedure because it seemed to be the fastest route to recovery. I also learned that my body would heal faster if surgeons used my own tissue in place of metallic or synthetic parts.

After the bone grafting procedure was completed, the surgeons needed to remove the external fixation rods screwed into my bone that exited my leg and were attached to a stabilizing structure outside it. That process would take some time as my leg first needed to completely heal from the bone graft surgery.

The healing process following my bone graft procedure was extensive and exhausting. Between surgeries, my days at the hospital became routine and regimented. I woke up, had breakfast, and then did physical and occupational therapy almost every morning. I returned to my room for lunch and then accepted visitors or watched television. My wife brought me plenty of DVDs to help pass the time. Occasionally, the medical staff made rounds to perform minor check-ups on my leg and hand to ensure they were both healing properly.

The Last Stop: Transition to Fisher House

Just as I was getting settled back into my routine, my doctor decided it was time for me to transition from Walter Reed to the Fisher House, a step-down facility where soldiers undergo therapy and treatment on an outpatient basis. Although "graduating" to the Fisher House was a huge milestone in my recovery, I wasn't quite ready to go. I believed I needed more time for my leg to heal from the bone graft procedure. I was also worried about the threat of infection and the dire, life-altering consequences that came with it. I didn't want to lose my leg, especially after all of the painful rehabilitation I'd done up to that point.

My doctor was not thrilled to hear that I wasn't in a hurry to transition to the Fisher House. I had Iisha's support and she agreed that the hospital would be the best place for me until my leg was healed. With her set to return home to Ohio, she felt more comfortable with me remaining at Walter Reed in her absence. It was obvious that this particular doctor was used to getting his way, as he dismissively continued to pressure me into going to the Fisher House. At the height of his frustration, he announced his plans to take me off Dilaudid, a potent opioid I'd been prescribed for pain management for the past two and half months. I found it strange that the doctor suddenly decided to take me off of Dilaudid when I refused to adhere to his medical advice. His decision, in my mind, was clearly borne out of retaliation for me resisting his plans.

Prior to nearly losing my leg, I'd never indulged in any hard-core drugs, so I'd become dependent on the Dilaudid for pain management. Given the extent of my injuries, keeping my pain under control was paramount to my recovery. Consequently, my pain management program left me in a vulnerable place to develop an addiction to Dilaudid. I felt like my vulnerability was being exploited and the humiliation was uncomfortable to deal with. Ultimately, I took the doctor's sudden decision as a slap in the face; his subtle way of punishing me for my defiance.

Although I was aware of the possible withdrawal side effects, I wasn't ready for what would happen to me once the medication left my system for good. At first, the medical staff administered my pain meds through an IV. Some of the nurses had trouble accessing the veins in my arms, which impacted my treatment. There were days that I didn't receive my pain meds on schedule. On one glorious, rainy morning, my nurse came in for my routine IV site change but there was nothing routine about that particular morning. The nurse mistook me for a human pin cushion from her multiple failed attempts to find a vein. At the time, I was recovering from one of my surgeries and was too weak to scream or even speak out in protest of being jabbed repeatedly. To make matters worse, my injured arm throbbed due to the nurse's inability to administer my pain meds. Both arms were shot, and I wasn't a very happy camper.

Sick of the nurses not being able to find a vein to administer the medication I desperately needed, I requested to have an arterial line installed on that same day. There were significant risks associated with having a line installed, but after that morning's adventure, I figured I'd take my chances. They threaded the line through an artery in my left bicep, which ran toward my heart. With the line installed, I had the ability to administer a dose of Dilaudid every ten minutes with the press of a button. The goal of the arterial line was to give me more control over my medication dosage, or at least I thought. As it turns out, my discomfort led to the drug taking control of me. I felt like this created an opportunity for the doctor to use my addiction as a chess piece to manipulate me. Initially, I dismissed the doctor's threat of taking me off Dilaudid as empty words.

"Do what you gotta do," I said. "But I'm staying in this hospital and in this room for another few weeks. I don't need this little funky medicine."

Boy, was I in for a rude awakening. I had no clue how powerful and malevolent the withdrawal symptoms would be or about the unrelenting agony I would suffer because of it. While engaging in a war of wills with the doctor, I'd failed to realize that I'd given myself a dose of Dilaudid every ten minutes for three straight months. The only exception was the few hours I was in therapy, but I usually received a boost prior to going in order to help push me through the session. My doctor knew that I should have been weaned off the medicine well before that point. I guess since he thought I was being difficult and non-compliant, he felt the need for me to quit the drug *cold turkey* in order to transition to Fisher House, which was pretty cold-hearted of him. My main concern about being transferred to Fisher House was the lack of support and no longer having round-the-clock nurse care. I didn't feel as though I were ready to be fully on my own yet.

They gave me my final push of Dilaudid before therapy. I know, cruel right? Afterward, I returned to my room, just in time for lunch. I was doing fine without the Dilaudid IV for a while, but a few hours after my last dose, things started to get real. My body began craving it and I quickly entered the withdrawal stage. Apparently, pushing a button that feeds you an opioid every 10 minutes can become quite addictive. I've seen withdrawal scenes portrayed in movies and

TV shows before and it just looked like dramatized "acting". Well, I'm here to tell you, I could have won an Academy Award for my "performance", but every bit of it was real.

When you have no idea whether you're hot or cold and you feel like you're sweating and itching incessantly, the physical side effects can easily begin to affect your mental state. At first, I was unaware of my withdrawal symptoms because it was a new experience for me. I had no idea how to handle what I was experiencing or how to make the sensations go away. So, I suffered in silence in my room for about an hour and a half, attempting to read, watch TV, rest, and walk around. I tried to do whatever I could to take my mind off the fact that I had no control over what was happening to me. I felt completely helpless again, just like the day of the bombing. The withdrawal experience was mind-boggling and I had no clue what was happening to me. So, I did the one thing that I knew would help bring me some peace; I called Iisha. When she answered the phone, I immediately broke down into tears. Emotions overtook me as I tried to explain my symptoms to her.

She calmly replied, "Oh baby, you're just having withdrawals from the drug." I remembered thinking, *withdrawal? I ain't no drug addict!* As my advocate, it didn't matter if she was physically present or not. Iisha called the nurse's desk to inform them of my situation. The nurses came rushing to my room to assess the situation and assist me. In true drug-addict form, my initial response wasn't my best. Once I laid eyes on them, I begged for "just a little bit more" of the Dilaudid to take the edge off. I bargained, "You know, just enough to get me through the night."

As I think back on that moment, I know that a life involving addiction was not for me. After examining me, they finally gave me some more of the medicine to wean me off, as my previous medical staff should have done. After the medicine hit my bloodstream, I eventually began to feel better. That entire night, I ended up tossing and turning and getting very little sleep. The pain in my legs and hand wasn't unbearable, but my body was working to push the Dilaudid out of my system. It was a full five days later before I shook the withdrawal effects and began feeling normal again. I was relieved to finally be able to sleep again. With that traumatic experience behind me, I had 20/20 vision regarding the situation. I realized that the horror stories I'd heard about drug addiction and vets were very real and that it was a path I knew I could never go down again.

FIVE

When revisiting my dreams of competing in the Olympics prior to enlisting in the Army, I have fond memories of watching track and field athlete Angelo Taylor competing in 2008. I was inspired while learning about his comeback story. It fueled my passion to train as hard as I could in order to see if I really had what it took to make it as far as the Olympics. In Iraq, all I'd done was train after my missions and daily tasks were completed. I was a solid 200 pounds and had been in great physical condition. Unfortunately, the bombing happened and dashed my dreams of making the Olympics.

During my first three months at Walter Reed, I had very little movement ability and exercise was out. As a result, my body mass began to shrink because the body only needs enough muscle for daily functions. Any other mass that you acquire is used by the body to heal and repair itself. In the nine months I spent at Walter Reed, I lost over 70 pounds. I hadn't been that small since 8th grade. This was a mental struggle for me because, ever since the age of 14, I'd been a gym rat. Working out helped build up my self-confidence as a teen and the gym remained a staple in my life as a place of peace and comfort.

On most days, it was hard to look in the mirror. Looking at my physical injuries was difficult because they symbolized the independence and normalcy that was taken from me. Although I made it a point to smile and keep up appearances for my wife and kids, I often cried to myself while alone because of how I still struggled.

No matter how I tried to encourage myself, I found myself mentally vulnerable to my demons as they constantly attacked me. I tried to focus on the positive things that were still happening in my life. I still had my life and my family. I'd made future plans to move forward with my life. But I still contended with some serious self-limiting beliefs. Over my lifetime, I'd struggled with self-esteem issues growing up. Some of them were due to internal insecurities and others were based on my physical appearance, like the fact that I'd been teased for having a large nose.

In some aspects, the older I got, the more I'd learned to accept myself. I'd built my personality and self-esteem around having an athletic physique. Being fit and active in sports were my ways of escaping any areas where I felt I'd fallen short in the looks department. So, you can safely assume that being blown apart didn't do much to help that situation. Even though I knew my wife wasn't shallow enough to base my worth on my appearance, my injuries still renewed my fear of abandonment caused by my missing my mother at a young age. Furthermore, it was common to hear about a spouse leaving a partner who'd served in the military and experienced a drastic shift in their lifestyle. Most spouses or caregivers felt overwhelmed by the huge responsibility and ultimately decided they couldn't deal with it. But, like the excellent wife she'd always proven herself to be, Iisha assured me that she would be right there to help me rebuild and bounce back even stronger. Now that I think about it, I don't know what I was worried about.

During the first three months of my rehabilitation process, my wife, kids, and father traveled back and forth from Ohio to D.C to visit me. My wife brought one of our sons at a time to provide the opportunity for one-on-one father bonding and quality time. She was working on her master's degree at the time, so life had become quite stressful for her. We also had some critical decisions ahead of us regarding the details of our future. I would soon move from the hospital to the Fisher House in Maryland. The Fisher House is a charity and foundation that provides complimentary housing for military and veteran's families for the duration of a loved one's hospital stay or treatment plan. We began weighing all of our options and the biggest one concerned moving the family to Maryland. We knew I couldn't go to the Fisher House alone while I was still in external fixation, relying on a wheelchair, and unable to walk for extended periods. I would need constant help, but we didn't feel comfortable uprooting my family and having no other local support for the kids at that time.

I've had a handful of friends that I can count on, regardless of the circumstances. My best friend, Dave, was in Korea at the time so I called on my other best friend, Miguel. My dire need at that time taught me just how rare true friendship is.

I sent Miguel a simple text that said, *I need someone to come stay with me for a while at the hospital. Can you help out?*

He replied, *I got you brother, get me all the details.*

Problem solved.

Life in the Fisher House Begins

Within a matter of days, the military made arrangements to bring my boy to D.C. Upon his arrival, I was packed up and ready to face the next phase of my adventure of recovery as the newest resident at the Fisher House. Experiencing life at the veteran medical center with Miguel was great, but it was also one hell of an adventure. He accompanied me to every physical and occupational therapy session and each doctor appointment. Miguel always made sure my meds were filled and that I had everything I needed. His friendship and support played a major role in my progression while living there.

In the meantime, my military unit's homecoming was approaching and it was important for me to be there to experience that moment with them. I worked tirelessly at improving my mobility skills as my goal was to be able to walk comfortably in front of my comrades. Plus, while in the hospital, conversing with my platoon members, I told each of them that I wasn't going to make the event. I was planning to make my surprise appearance there a memorable moment for everyone. During the early days of physical therapy, I used a special walker that allowed me to rest my arm on a secured pad. Eventually, I mastered using the walker and showed a lot of improvement before graduating to crutches. I enjoyed this stage of walking the least because I hated having those crutches jammed in my armpits. Once my walking continued to improve, my therapist cleared me to finally use a cane one week before my unit was scheduled to come home.

Of course, being hospitalized didn't override my Army status, so I still had to apply for leave whenever I wanted to leave. Ten months passed since I last saw my home and I couldn't wait to get back to clear my head. Being a long-term hospital resident had been challenging and I looked forward to having some normalcy in my life. I was also hopeful of finding peace with some of the demons that had plagued me for the four months I'd spent in the hospital.

Homecoming and Redemption

My first homecoming was in October of 2009. My unit had finally returned home and the 135th Military Police unit was about to get a pleasant surprise. I'd coordinated everything with the home unit for my entrance and return. I was proud to be able to stand on my own two feet and show all my family, friends, and fellow soldiers that this improvised explosive device (IED) didn't take me down. It was important for me to give hope to my brothers and sisters that had returned home that they, too, could face the battle and return strong. I know their battles weren't physical like mine, but the mental and emotional stress battle can also be tough to deal with.

When I arrived at Kenston High School, they hid me in a side office as everyone filed into the gym. During that time, I was greeted by many of the higher-ups in the Ohio National Guard. They all showed their appreciation and respect for everything that I endured. They commended me for pushing myself so that I could be there that day. As I sat in that office, I heard Scottish bagpipes play the Army song and it triggered sentimental memories. A strong sense of pride and joy overtook me because I'd served in the greatest Army in the world. I survived a blast that would have killed most men. For a moment, I felt peace consume me for the first time and it became clear to me that moving forward wouldn't be as difficult as I'd originally thought.

The gym was filled with family and friends who hadn't seen their loved ones in months. I saw my unit sitting on the gym floor, ready to be welcomed back and to finally close out their mission. I slowly crept out and hid alongside the bleachers in the back while our battalion commanding officer made the introduction.

"It wouldn't be right if we didn't have *all* the members of the 135th Military Police company here with us today. After months of rehab and surgeries, he has pushed himself to be here today. Please welcome Sergeant Corwyn Collier!"

I began slowly making my way to the front of the gym with the use of my cane as the crowd erupted with cheers. The Army song blared out louder than before and my whole unit rose to their feet as I walked down the aisle. I smiled and waved with a joy-filled heart, once again feeling like I was a part of something bigger than myself. I joined my brothers and sisters, proud that we'd all made it back home - no matter the outcome - we'd all made it.

The ceremony proceeded and I received multiple awards commending my service. Amongst all of them, my Purple Heart pinning ceremony meant the most to me. My drill sergeant had previously mentioned how respected the Purple Heart award was, but it was least coveted because earning it meant that you were injured in combat. But I was pretty damn proud to receive it in person. I'd initially received it via mail in a biohazard bag with my dog tags and wedding ring. Attending the ceremony served as closure for that mission and everything else that had taken place in my life since the explosion. It symbolized my leadership, my courage, and my duty to my country, my squad, and my team.

Once the ceremony ended, I was swarmed by family and fellow soldiers, and it felt good to be surrounded by people who were so happy to see me alive and well. I was interviewed by several newspapers about my experience in the military and my active recovery journey. Afterward, I went home and enjoyed my family for a few weeks after nearly a year of separation. I spent time catching up with friends and family who weren't able to make it to D.C. I was grateful to be back home and experience a daily routine that didn't involve nurses, doctors, and long hospital halls. Spending time with just my wife and kids and returning to our life as we had always known it was deeply meaningful for me. But, like all good things, my visit home had to come to an end and I needed to return to Walter Reed. Although I had to leave my family behind again, I was more motivated and determined to kick physical therapy and occupational therapy in the ass.

SIX

I was still in my external fixator and I had a lot more to accomplish in my recovery plan before I could return home for good. So, when I returned to Walter Reed, I had a renewed motivation to restart my therapy routine. My passion to walk into my homecoming ceremony had previously fueled my efforts to reach a significant milestone. Being home gave me the opportunity to reset my mind and create new goals and opportunities for myself. So, I was focused on crossing the finish line.

Getting up for therapy no longer felt like a chore. I viewed it like practicing for the big game - the game of getting back home. I knew my family needed me, and although my wife was successfully juggling everything at home - finishing a master's degree, working a new teaching job, moving into a new home, and keeping the boys together - she still needed my support. So, on mornings when I felt a little tired or a little depressed, I pressed on because I knew I could no longer feel sorry for myself. Not as long as my wife was still carrying the load on her own.

I can honestly say that I can be pretty forgetful about some minor responsibilities in my life. One of those things, while I was at the

Fisher House, was the task of recharging my electric wheelchair. Due to my hand injury, I couldn't use a regular wheelchair to get around and I wasn't quite strong enough to walk for long periods of time without frequent breaks. So I required a motorized wheelchair for any errands or tasks that required extended use of my time. On one particular day, Miguel and I were out running our usual errands and going to appointments when we realized I'd forgotten to charge my chair the night before. As we were making our way back to the Fisher House, it died on me. Just to set the scene properly, a motorized wheelchair is far from light and the Walter Reed campus is far from small. The only option we had for getting me back home was for Miguel, who is not the biggest guy in the world, to push me all the way back in the chair. It's a good thing he wasn't a sucker. He put in work gritting and grinding all the way back and returned me safely to my room. This was another grateful moment that showed me his true friendship. That act solidified the fact that we were tied for life. Miguel was definitely my ride-or-die during that difficult time.

When the United Service Organizations (USO) of Cincinnati invited my family out for a weekend festival, I made sure that Miguel joined us. We had the privilege of being flown there from D.C. on a private jet. Coming up the way I had, being on a private jet was an experience of a lifetime that I never thought I'd have. The interior was everything you could imagine and was true to what you've probably seen on TV and in movies. It was nice to experience that kind of treatment. I only wished my wife could have experienced it with me.

Upon arrival in Cincinnati, as we exited the jet, a high school band played the Army song for us. Let's just say your boy felt quite presidential at that moment. It was like my own private homecoming ceremony. Afterward, a limo drove us to one of the nicest hotels in downtown Cincinnati where my family was waiting for me. I was greeted by my wife and kids, father, mother-in-law, and all my siblings. It was a joyous occasion, to say the least. The weekend activities included dinners, meet and greets with local businessmen and women, a mix of celebrities, and many opportunities for me to share brief parts of my story. Being in my family's presence again filled my spirit with hope, as they've always been my source of motivation. Each milestone I've hit and recognition I've ever achieved feels sweeter with them celebrating by my side.

Eyes on the Prize

As time went on, I knew that Miguel's time with me at the hospital was coming to an end. I would need all the strength I could muster to make it through the last few months alone. In mid-November, it was time for Miguel to leave. Although my wife was worried about me being at Fisher House on my own, I knew I would be okay. I had my schedule down pat and I'd learned how to utilize the campus transportation system to get from the Fisher House to Walter Reed's main hospital. I couldn't afford to have any more wheelchair battery issues since I was now riding solo, so I'd become more responsible when it came to making sure all my ducks were in a row.

I pretty much kept to myself, spending countless hours in my room watching movies and playing video games since I'd never really made friends at the hospital. On most days, I felt alone. Although there were numerous activities offered by the hospital and ways to get involved with the community, I only recall doing a couple that I enjoyed, both sporting events. One was attending a Georgetown game and the other was a Wizards game. When the winter months came, I gradually grew more depressed. My body mass was still shrinking, there was no definitive day that I would get the external fixator off, my family was far away, and the only happiness I experienced was during therapy, which only accounted for two hours of my day.

To extend my endorphin high, I eventually got an exercise band to try and exercise in my room with a few movements to help rebuild my arm, back, and shoulder strength. Over time, it became more evident that I only had the use of one thumb, so the manner of lifting things would become more difficult. I decided to sit down with my occupational therapist to begin looking into ways to reestablish my grip. Walter Reed had engineered some of the most unique prosthetics I'd ever seen. We came up with a game plan to create a casing that would go over my hand with an extended curve resembling fingers to fit around the bars. The goal was to give it a test run after I returned to Walter Reed from my Christmas leave.

December finally arrived and I was excited to return home and spend Christmas with my family. To add to my excitement, I received unexpected news from my doctors. They'd finally concluded that my leg was strong enough to remove the external fixator before I went home. I was ready to go into the home stretch. After countless x-rays and constant procedures with adding the missing bone, it was time for the final part of my recovery. The removal was an easy outpatient surgery. Although my leg hadn't fully healed, it damn sure felt great to look down and no longer see an iron cage around it. I definitely wasn't going to miss it, nor the extended airport check-in process that came along with it. I was looking forward to the option of a sleeping position other than on my back, which I'd been doing for the past seven months. I was also excited to do basic things like wear jeans instead of relying on tear-away basketball pants.

I believed the physical transition was going to be amazing, but I also had serious concerns. As much as I wanted to be able to stand on my own feet and be strong, my leg was much smaller after the procedure and the extent of muscle damage terrified me. I'd seen and heard stories of people who'd tried to save their leg only to still lose it due to infections or the leg's inability to help support their body weight. All that remained of my leg was tibia and less than half of my calf muscle. My doctors instructed me to wear an air cast boot while walking for protection. But, due to underlying fear, I continued to rely on my wheelchair to get around. Ultimately, I was afraid of losing my leg and even more afraid of prolonging my hospital stay. Since I yearned to be home with my family more than anything, I did everything I could to protect that opportunity.

Nonetheless, when the time came for me to return home for Christmas leave, the string of bad news was relentless. Because D.C. and the surrounding areas were hit with a massive snowstorm, all of the inbound flights were canceled. A few days before Christmas, I was stuck at the Fisher House with no way home. In tears, I called my wife with the bad news because it would be our family's first Christmas apart.

All she said was, "Shid! Honey, Ross and I will be on our way to come and get you. I've got four-wheel drive on my Jeep. I've got this."

Unfortunately, the snowstorm wasn't only bad in the D.C. area. It had hit the entire east coast and parts of the Midwest. However, it was no match for my wife who was determined to get me home for Christmas. I was concerned for her safety but also excited that my wife had taken such a huge risk to make sure I was home with my family for the holidays. She quickly packed and immediately set out to make the expedition to D.C. On average, it takes about five and half hours to reach Walter Reed from Akron, but the snowstorm slowed her down tremendously. She didn't arrive until later that evening.

We packed the car with my belongings and soon, we were on the road to get me back home to see my boys. It was my first road trip since the accident and the removal of the external fixator couldn't have had better timing. I could sit comfortably for the extended ride in the car. We were about halfway through the journey when it grew too dark and snowy to keep going. We called it a night and stopped at a hotel in Pennsylvania. Early the next morning, we hit the road again and several hours later, we were home. I was thrilled to see my family and had also planned to purchase a new car for myself through a grant I'd received from a program at Walter Reed.

It was a big deal for me because I'd never owned a car as a teenager. I'd either walk, catch a ride with friends, or use my dad's spare car for wherever I needed to go. When I finally graduated college, I had such poor credit, I was forced to go to a buy-here-pay-here lot, similar to the one Matilda's dad ran. I bought a 2000 Dodge Stratus with more miles on it than the stretch of the U.S. I can't lie, it was a piece of shit. But, no matter the circumstances, I'd gotten it on my own. That Dodge gave me hell for years until it broke down, right before my deployment. So, getting a new car after struggling for four years with that car felt like fate.

As a result of my time in Iraq, I'd developed PTSD and was triggered by certain things while I was at home. One thing that affected my mental health involved the manner in which I traveled. I only felt safe while riding in vehicles that stood high off the ground, like trucks and SUVs. This impacted the details of my car search.

Although my right leg was still recovering and gaining strength, I hadn't yet been cleared to drive. But I knew I wanted to buy an SUV. So, a few days before Christmas, the wife and I headed over to the car lot and we purchased my second vehicle, a 2010 Jeep Commander. I couldn't believe that after the "struggle years" I'd suffered with my other vehicle, I could finally afford to buy something I truly wanted in life. I was grateful for the grant as well as my wife's commitment to clean up my credit while I was away.

It goes without saying that Christmas of 2009 was one to remember, and not only because I was able to spend quality time with a variety of family and friends. The highlight of my time at home was being able to see my sons open all of their gifts. On this particular Christmas, the boys were chosen by the Chagrin Falls police department to participate in their annual Christmas shopping spree. It was their way of showing gratitude for my service since our National Guard unit was located in their neighborhood. So let's just say, due to the contributions from the police department and my wife and I, we had the happiest five and two-year-olds in the city of Akron.

Far too soon, my visit home came to an end, once again. My family helped me celebrate my 28th birthday and within a week, I was back on a flight to Walter Reed, this time alone. Returning to the Fisher House without my family or Miguel was a lonely experience. I spent most of my time sitting in my room and feeling sorry for myself regarding my situation. But one day, all of it changed and I'll never forget how it happened. For a brief moment in time, a light switch flipped inside of me. It had been well over a month since my external fixator was removed from my leg, yet I was still rolling around in a wheelchair. At an appointment, my occupational therapist watched me roll into the room and asked, "CJ, why the hell are you still in that thing?"

As I looked down at myself, I honestly couldn't answer her. I'd had an air cast that I used for short distances, like walking down to the food court in the Fisher house. I'd also walked during physical therapy sessions almost every other day. But I was still afraid to release my safety net. That's when she said, "After this weekend, I don't want to see you in that chair anymore. You cried and whined about wanting to walk on your own. You said you wanted to run one day. That ain't gonna happen from there!"

Sometimes we just need to hear things spoken aloud that we know are true, deep down inside. When someone places a mirror in front of you, you have to face yourself and admit that you have flaws. I realized I was still suffering from depression and I knew that was a large part of my resistance to physical progression. Just like that, a simple conversation with her gave me the confidence I needed. I returned the borrowed wheelchair to the hospital that same week and I never looked back.

My determination to walk on my own two feet was renewed. Over time, I grew comfortable enough with the air cast to make trips to the mall. I preferred new scenery and pushing myself out of my comfort zone. My goal was still to return home for good and I knew I'd have to prove that I was capable of taking care of myself. I also had to prove that my body was strong enough to function without additional surgery. When my walking continued to improve, my physical therapist finally agreed that I no longer needed the air cast. I was ready to transition into an ankle-foot orthosis brace (AFO). This was a simple device that would wrap around my leg and slide into my shoe to provide extra support while walking. It would be a game-changer because it would aid my driving process as well.

Meanwhile, the pressure to get home continued to build. Iisha was doing her best to tread above water with her new teaching job and caring for a five and two-year-old alone. I felt helpless and guilty during most of our phone calls for allowing this inconvenience to happen to our family. The mounting stress from my situation was eating me alive daily. I knew I had to figure out a way to return home and support my family.

I finally had a conversation with my commander and requested placement at a Warrior Transition Unit. From there, I would be able to complete my rehabilitation process near home. Although she was reluctant, my commander agreed to transition me and allow me to return to Ohio to be with my family. Then I would await my medical board's approval for Army and VA benefits. They found a doctor and a physical therapist within minutes of my home and, on March 10, 2010, I finally said goodbye to Walter Reed for good.

Returning home was a feeling like no other. Although my time at Walter Reed felt like it had taken forever, I'd actually beaten the doctor's original recovery timetable of 15 months in almost half the time. I'd made it out of there in only 9 months.

SEVEN

Of course, returning home had stipulations attached since I was still enlisted in the Army. I was required to make all scheduled physical and occupational therapy appointments, as well as report to my National Guard unit each day. I was just grateful to be home at first, so it didn't really impact me. Then I began growing bored with having to report to the office just to shred paper or sit around all day because it was my "duty".

Eventually, I learned to make the best of that boredom. My unit provided a small weight room for full-time people to remain active and fit. This would be the perfect assist in my rehab process and also served as a way for me to gain a little weight back. So I began a new journey of incorporating daily fitness into my life. Monday through Friday, I would hit the weights and develop routines and lifts to accommodate my new body. Lifting became a passion of mine a few short weeks later and it also focused my mind on the right things until I started school.

During my time at the unit, I decided to attend The University of Akron, where my wife had earned both her bachelors and masters degrees. Iisha's contacts put me in touch with the military program on campus. I wasn't sure which kind of teacher I wanted to be at first. I was considering elementary and secondary school. But, if I'm being one-hundred percent honest, elementary school wasn't a realistic option for me. After seeing my wife handle the complications of dealing with such little ones, I knew there was no damn way I had the patience to manage that type of career.

I began looking into secondary education and explored my subject options. Math originally crossed my mind until I looked at the required courses and it instantly became a *hell no* for me. Science was too complex and well, let's face it, English can be rather boring in high school. Due to some excellent teachers I had while growing up, I always had a love for history. So, I figured I'd give it a try. After going through all of the proper channels with the school and Veterans Affairs, in May of 2010, I was officially enrolled and starting my first summer term at The University of Akron. Since I was a full-time student, I was no longer required to report to my unit. I looked forward to only focusing on school.

Starting classes was intimidating at first. Ironically, I graduated with my bachelor's in May of 2005, and, five years later, I was back on a college campus. Although there were older people in my classes, I still felt like the old guy. I also lacked confidence whenever I was in public. At Walter Reed, I fit in because to some degree, we'd all had injuries and we were usually missing parts that we'd been born with because of the war. But in the world, that comfort blanket no longer existed for me. Most of the time, I wore a hoodie or sweats while on campus to hide my disfigurement. When people stared at me, although I couldn't read their minds, I couldn't help but wonder what they were thinking or saying to each other. It isn't like I had a giant sign over my head explaining that I'd been injured while in combat. All they could see was missing fingers and a mangled right leg. I felt uneasy and like a "freak".

This feeling transcended beyond school. Whenever I attended any type of public outing or function, I kept my hand in my pocket and always wore jeans during those hot summer days because I was insecure about the way I might look to others. It wasn't until I went to Arizona to visit friends and to attend my frat brother's wedding that I finally overcame my fear of what people thought of my appearance. That Arizona heat makes a man come to his senses and I realized that I couldn't allow my fear of the outside world's perception to make me feel insecure about the wounds I endured while fighting for my country. During that vacation, I wore shorts in public for the first time since the injury. I felt relieved because I'd gotten out of my own head and gained a little of my life back. Although my advance force operations (AFO) had a Purple Heart sticker on the back just to help ease my mind, I was making progress.

Though I was making progress and shedding some insecurities about my physical appearance, memories from the explosion were still fresh in my mind. It had only been a year since the incident. One of the things I loved about The University of Akron was its beautiful campus and diverse population of students. One afternoon as I was headed to class, there was a group of gentlemen nearby speaking a foreign language. I hadn't heard Arabic being spoken since my accident, but I instantly recognized it. I can vividly remember how I froze in my steps and the architecture of the surrounding buildings and streets immediately morphed into the ones I remembered seeing in Iraq. A chill consumed my spine as I instantly grew nervous and scared. At that moment, I couldn't decide whether to retreat to my car or quickly get to the building ahead of me. I dashed inside the building and quickly made my way to class in hopes that I would soon forget about the incident. Eventually, I was able to see the group of gentlemen as innocent people and not as possible terrorists who I'd have to defend myself and others against.

Later that summer, I experienced another fear-induced incident. The 4th of July was approaching and, as usual, fireworks were sporadically used in the neighborhood throughout the week. One day, while I was at Dairy Queen ordering ice cream for my family, an incident took place that I'll never forget. Right next to the Dairy Queen drive-through was a barber shop with a group of teenage boys standing outside. They were just having fun, or so I thought. As I pulled up to the window to pay for my ice cream, a loud explosion went off and I instantly felt like I was back in May of 2009. I hit the gas on my Hummer and flew into traffic, barely avoiding a collision before racing back home. My heart was racing and I was overtaken by a rush of adrenaline. I immediately took my phone out and called my wife.

"Iisha it's happening again! They're trying to take me out!" I yelled.

Iisha asked, "Who? What happened? Why are you breathing so hard?"

"An explosive just went off beside my car!" I said.

She told me to calm down and to drive home safely so we could talk.

Once I made it home, she assured me that I was overreacting and that I was going to be okay. But in my mind, it wasn't a year ago that a bomb went off by my truck. It felt like only a few weeks ago. I was still dealing with the aftermath and mentally recovering from it. The harder I tried to move on from it, the more the details of the event haunted me. I was even afraid of riding in cars that didn't sit high up because not being able to see the road from an elevated position made me uneasy.

Despite the incident, I still decided to go to attend a 4th of July celebration in Akron. Needless to say, the post-traumatic stress continued. My wife and kids wanted to experience the Red, White, and Blue festival at Lock 3 Park. We also wanted to support a family friend who would have a food truck at the event. I figured it wouldn't be so bad and, for precaution, I brought my headphones to help block some of the unexpected noises. When the fireworks began, at first, I seemed to be doing okay. But as the blasts grew more and more intense, I realized I couldn't handle it anymore. I eventually covered my head with my hoodie and put on my headphones while patiently waiting for it to end. This was when I realized I needed assistance with coping. I'd been laser-focused on my physical recovery process but I'd never taken the time to work on the mental healing journey that was also required.

While I was in the hospital, I always shrugged off the mental impact of the incident as no big deal. I never wanted to be viewed by others as weak or to allow PTSD to control me. But what I failed to realize was there was no way to overcome or conquer something I'd never dealt with before without acknowledging its existence. It took a lot from me, along with some encouragement from my wife to seek help. I eventually started seeing a therapist who helped me work through the mental aspects of the trauma I'd experienced. Those therapy sessions were much needed and helped me regain a piece of my life I thought I'd lost forever.

As I began doing the work with my therapy, life began moving along great. Iisha and I never had the chance to have an official wedding ceremony, so we made it a priority to finally have the one we'd always wanted. We set a date - July 30th, 2010 - to celebrate our love for each other and the fact that I was still alive. In preparation,

I began increasing my effort in rehab by going to the gym five days a week in addition to physical and occupational therapy. My goal was to dance with my bride and step my ass off with my fraternity brothers to give everyone the ultimate comeback show. So, when I say I busted my ass for those months leading up to the wedding, I left nothing up to chance.

Our wedding was undoubtedly one of the biggest highlights of those first few months back home. I was blessed to be surrounded by family, high school and college friends, and my military family. I'd accomplished my goal of having enough physical strength in my leg to be able to groove with my wife and hit that good ol' Alpha train with the bruhs. It was a night I would never forget and it gave me a small piece of my life back.

As the year came to an end, I had successfully completed my summer and fall semesters. My therapy sessions were almost over, but I was still trying to find peace within myself. I still lacked self-confidence in my appearance and was still hesitant to be myself around others. I would only wear shorts with a military hat or some type of shirt so people could put two and two together. But the more I went to the gym - during therapy and afterward - I realized I'd found a place that I was 100% confident in. The hours I spent at the gym gave me something nothing else could give me at that time, and that was peace. It became more than just a way to build my body back up, but a place where I found the old me, the whole me. As my size increased, so did my strength and I could look around the gym and see that I was just like everyone else there. It was a wonderful feeling. I eventually spent the majority of my time in school, working out, and being a father and husband.

The time kept pushing along and life seemed to improve as I continued to navigate through being a stay-at-home dad and student. All the while, I was waiting to be processed out of the Army. For Easter of 2011, we decided to take the boys on a staycation to Kalahari resort in Sandusky, Ohio. Little did we know, we were in for a surprise that weekend. On our first day there, Iisha was feeling a little off. It was a feeling that she was familiar with, so she asked me to run to the store and grab a pregnancy test. Lo and behold, the test read positive…and our family of four was now looking to add its fifth member! Now, as excited as I was to have my third child, I was also terrified. With the physical changes I'd recently undergone, how would my child perceive me? Would my hand scare him or her? It was already mentally difficult for me to deal with these concerns with my other two children, so I wasn't sure if I could do it again. But Iisha pointed out two key things to help reassure me that our child would love me no matter what. First, she reminded me of what our older son, Malachi, had shared with me. She said, "Remember how he told you he was going to be an engineer and find a way to give you back your hand and leg?" Then she reminded me how Corwyn only cared that I could still pick him up and sit him on my lap. She reassured me that our unborn child would only know this version of me and would love ME because I am their father. Those words helped me tremendously moving forward and helped me to continue to strive to accept myself and my injuries.

On November 30th, 2011, our third son, Aaron, was born. We purchased a new home and I was entering my final year of college. My mental and physical advancements were steady and I was headed into another chapter of life, two years removed from the accident. At the beginning of 2012, I received a phone call from my former high school teacher informing me that I'd been selected for a Pathfinder award for their upcoming Black History month program. I was surprised to receive such an honor, considering the caliber of recipients before me. It was great to stand in front of a large group of kids and tell them about my struggles and how I'd reached this point in my life. At the end of my speech, I left them with two quotes, one was original and the other was what my wife used to say to me all the time.

First, I told them, "Don't let your current situation dictate your future." I chose this quote because of the significance of my healing journey after the accident. Plenty of times, I'd felt defeated and believed the road ahead of me was too difficult to bear. But, with the right support and mindset, I'd managed to persevere and reach a positive point in my life. The second quote, from Iisha was, "It's not about the disability, it's the ability." I've lived by these two quotes and whenever I was down, they reminded me of who I was during my struggle.

Little did I know, my biggest challenge was still on the horizon.

EIGHT

I was completing my master's program and it was finally time to begin student teaching. I'd recently completed classroom observation hours and even had the opportunity to teach a lesson. So, getting up in front of a class wasn't foreign to me. But when the time came for all eyes to be on me, once again, I'll admit, I was in my feelings.

How would those kids react to seeing me and my hand?

We all know that the 7th through 12th grade years can be an interesting period in our lives. Sometimes people in this age range have no tact and lack filters. So, as the summer concluded and student teaching placements were assigned, I was nervous about finding out exactly where I'd be placed. When I finally received the email, I wasn't familiar with the area or the school. However, I was happy to be a part of Springfield Middle school under the guidance of Mrs. Elliott.

Student teaching was by far my favorite memory of earning my master's degree. I taught at a school with a student body from rural and urban communities. The school was predominantly white and

I was the only black staff member. I'm glad to say that all of the nervous energy I'd about being accepted went out the window after the first week of school. I shared my story with those kids and at that moment, they fell in love with me. I never realized how important building relationships was in education until I was in front of those kids in the classroom daily. They never once looked at me differently and the love and respect was reciprocated on both ends.

One of the key moments of my student teaching experience came on Veterans Day. For the first time since May 23, 2009, which was three years earlier, I'd put on my uniform and shared my story with the entire student body and staff. I finally realized that sharing who I was with people had become a critical part of my healing process. It was a way for me to show others how to transform pain into progress. On that day, we all gathered in the gymnasium and shared intimate details of my life with hundreds of middle school kids. The applause, the handshakes, and hugs exchanged that day showcased how blessed I was to still be here. I knew I'd found my purpose in life. On that day, God showed me that my story could help people, most importantly kids. As resilient as they are, they still need strong support in their lives to help them achieve success. I also caught the eye of several newspapers and was nominated for and won the Dr. James J. Sheehan Award for Pre-Service Social Studies Educator, making it the perfect celebration of Veterans Day.

My time at Springfield ended in December of 2012 and it was the hardest time I'd ever had saying goodbye. Those kids were my first students and I was the soldier who'd become their teacher. On my last day, tears flowed, laughs erupted, and tons of pictures were taken. Thankfully, it wasn't the last I'd seen of them. I occasionally subbed and helped with the track team since I'd graduated in the middle of the school year. I stayed in contact with my class over the years and even visited them in high school on occasion. I eventually attended their graduation in 2016 and was able to see the majority of them one last time. I'll always remember them for teaching me that heroes may physically change, but their spirit never dies.

The Mental and Physical Challenges Begin

In 2013, I was pushed mentally and physically to finally leave the details of what happened in Iraq in Iraq. My experience at Springfield inspired me to put myself and my story out there more. I learned to accept my injuries as a part of my story rather than wearing them in silent shame. That year, I submitted my story to editors at Men's Health magazine and Bodybuilding.com. Both editors were impressed by the advances I'd made in my physical recovery. They each offered me the opportunity to be featured on their platforms. I was thrilled at the opportunity to share what I'd accomplished over the years with others.

When I arrived home, I weighed 130 pounds. After years of training and keeping a strategic diet, I was 190 pounds. Going to the gym gave me the push I needed to remain consistent and focused. Over time, I no longer felt handicapped. Whenever I looked around the gym, I noticed that I was able to keep up with a lot of able-bodied people. This encouraged me to keep pushing beyond what my doctors predicted I'd be able to do. When I shared that insight with the editors at Men's Health magazine and Bodybuilding.com, they each put my story out there. The issue of Men's Health magazine featuring my story was released in March of 2013 and Bodybuilding. com arrived two months later in May, on the fifth anniversary of my Alive Day.

It was an incredible time for me because I was finally beginning to feel whole again. My social media followers began to climb and I was getting more opportunities to speak publicly about my life experiences. But notice I said I was *beginning* to feel whole. Despite the growing interest, support, and recognition I'd received, there was something still missing in my life.

I still needed a challenge to strive for through a healthy competitive outlet.

In 2013, I began looking more into paralympic sports to see if they offered powerlifting or even track events. I'd grown up competing, so it was a significant part of my identity. Hell, even the Army is a competition to get rank. But my push to find a competitive outlet was constantly met with a bunch of dead ends. I received little to no help with exploring what the military had to offer and I began to lose faith in finding a competitive program.

At that time, I was completely unaware that I'd pushed my body to the point where I was physically able to apply the pressure on my leg needed to run. My doctors had previously informed me that it wouldn't ever be possible for me to run. So naturally, I'd never attempted it. Most of the time, my cardio routine at the gym included using the elliptical or the bike because both machines required nothing more than the leg to maintain a rotating motion. Well, one spring afternoon, I was playing soccer in the backyard with my sons and doing my usual two-step hobble while trying to chase after them. Then, all of a sudden, they stopped in the middle of playing and said something to me that changed me forever.

"Dad, you can actually run," observed Malachi.

"Huh? Why do you say that?" I asked.

"Because we watched you out here with us and we can tell."

"Yeah, just go for it!" Corwyn Jr. encouraged me.

At that moment, I don't know if it was the love and rallying from my sons - who've been rocking with me since day one in the hospital - that gassed me up or some other source of inspiration. But, the next thing I knew, I was sprinting at full speed all over the yard. As I moved around confidently, I felt God's calming presence all over me. All the anger I'd felt because I believed He'd allowed my gifts to be snatched away from me faded. In actuality, God helped me appreciate what I had even more.

Although I was unsuccessful at finding a way to compete through the Paralympic and the military that summer, I was still able to get back on the track and run. Soon afterward, I signed up for a coach relay at one of my kids' track meets in Akron. I, along with Iisha and two other coaches, ran a 4x100 relay against other teams in the Lake Erie league for the Amateur Athletic Union (AAU). I was the team anchor. For the first time, everyone, including my father, would finally see the outcome of all of the work I'd been putting in over the past few months. I hadn't run track since 2005, but when that gun went off and the race started, I was transformed into my "old self".

I remember watching the first two legs run and I knew my wife was third, bringing it to me to finish. As I watched her get the baton and go, high school and college memories rushed through my head. The closer she got to me, the more I felt my heart racing with excitement. The next thing I knew, I was off running to get momentum. I was primed and ready to receive my exchange. When I heard that beautiful word "stick", I felt that baton pressed in my palm and I hauled ass down that home stretch. Riding on cloud nine, I couldn't believe I was back running on the track after all those years. After my doctors had told me that even walking was going to be a challenge for me, there I was, back in my element. I crossed the finish line and our team finished in third place. Just like that, the thrill of competing was reignited in me. It was great to be back on the track (pun intended) for that brief moment and I desired to give myself more of the thrill that accompanied that outlet. It was the one piece that I'd felt was missing during my recovery journey. Little did I know, I was about to find it.

Introduction to Bodybuilding

In late 2013, I was with my workout partner and high school friend, Nixon. He asked me a great question. "You're always in the gym. What's the end goal?"

Thrown off by his question, I couldn't answer him at the time. I wasn't sure what my purpose was. He whipped out his phone and said, "You should look into competing in men's physique."

I looked at him and said, "Who's about to put their blown-up ass on stage?"

As he laughed, he showed me a video of a men's bodybuilding competition. He informed me that they wore board shorts and that legs were not judged. As I watched the video, I was drawn to this new sport and was open to trying it out.

After doing some research on my own, I finally found a show to compete in, the Dave Liberman Natural Ohio in Cleveland. I'd been working out since high school, but I'd never trained to compete in a bodybuilding show. I knew nothing about nutrition or how to properly prepare for competitions. So I did what all rookies do. I went to bodybuilding.com and read articles about men's physique, diets, and different approaches to preparing for a show. I had 10 weeks to train before the next event. In the meantime, I had to learn how to balance my family, social life, work schedule, and training. It was a new experience that required me to combine life and military lessons. The road to the competition required restraint, passion, and commitment. There was a lot of personal sacrifice and discipline involved and it was challenging. But, for some reason, I wanted to see what the experience would be like. I needed that challenge after being home for almost four years after walking out of Walter Reed.

When the week of the show arrived, I still felt like a fish out of water. Sadly, I was still reading forums on bodybuilding.com and watching YouTube videos on posing. The sport was still fairly new at the time and they'd just named the first bodybuilding Olympian in 2013. So I was learning about competing essentials on the fly and had no idea how unprepared I was. I failed to obtain a National Physique Committee (NPC) card for competing in amateur bodybuilding events and I also lacked an understanding of how important tanning was for my appearance.

When I arrived at the hotel for check-in and tanning, the hotel was packed with fitness enthusiasts like me. I'd never seen anything like it, and I knew I was in for something special. Check-in was a breeze and tanning was a brand-new experience. Despite all of the training and preparation I'd undergone, deep down, I was still nervous about showing my leg on stage. I told myself that I needed this moment to feel complete again and I couldn't keep running from this moment. Although I'd had several breakthrough moments over the years, this was what I really needed in order to feel good about myself - no matter how people would perceive my body.

On Saturday, March 29, 2014, I walked into Lakewood High school auditorium for the athletes' meeting. There were trophies as tall as me on the stage. Seeing them brought on a feeling that I was where I was meant to be. After the athletes' meeting, I threw on my headphones and turned on Pandora. "Champion" by Kanye West was the first song to play and I definitely caught that sign.

Since I was brand new to the bodybuilding sport and had never watched any of the competitions firsthand, I had no idea how long the wait was for prejudging. I had very little food with me to make it through the day, so I sat and watched guys eat rice, sweet potatoes, beef, chicken, peanut butter, honey, jam, and rice cakes, while I chilled with nothing. Luckily, Nixon was coming to the show, so I asked him to bring me some rice cakes and peanut butter. As the hours passed by, I ate, exercised, and posed in the mirror because that was what I saw the other guys doing. I lacked direction and was literally making the shit up as I sat there.

After hours of sitting around, they finally called the men's physique group backstage. Butterflies hit my stomach and I came alive right then and there. As my class was called to line up, I forgot all about my injuries. I was just excited to show the crowd the results of all my hard work. As the announcer read my bio, the crowd erupted with applause. They learned what happened to me in Iraq and couldn't believe that I was there competing that day. After I completed my individual routine, I was called out and compared with the top five. After a few minutes of comparisons, they sent the five of us off the stage. I had no idea what was going on, but the other guys were pretty excited and informed me that we were the top five contestants. That meant one of those trophies on the stage was mine.

I was completely stunned. Nothing pleased me more than to learn that the blown-up soldier and amateur contestant who'd never done anything like this before had made it to the top five! Now all I had to do was wait for finals to see how I'd placed overall. After a few more hours of waiting around, Iisha and my frat brother, Ramon, popped in for the finals. I was excited to see them because they'd missed the pre-judging and it was important for them to be there when I learned how I'd placed. Once again, I was backstage, preparing to get back on stage for the finals. I couldn't believe how far I'd come from being a bedridden patient at the hospital, unable to stand on my own two feet, and slowly learning to walk again to becoming a men's physique competitor.

As the emcee began announcing the top five contestants, I watched them being dismissed from the lineup, one-by-one. My potential ranking went from fifth, to fourth, to third, until there were only two of us left standing on the stage in a battle for first place. I was nervous, excited, and stunned all at once. I'd come into this experience with no expectations about the outcome. I'd only wanted the chance to compete. As they announced the second-place contestant, my heart soared and I was overcome with emotion. With little to no knowledge about training, competing, and the bodybuilding industry, I'd won my very first competition in a men's physique show and became a national qualifier with an opportunity to battle for the overall title. Little did I know that in 2014, on that very stage in the midst of an overall battle, my future coach Gary Chaney was standing right up there with me.

I lost overall, but the Chicago competition was two and half months away. The possibility of becoming an International Federation of BodyBuilding and Fitness (IFBB) pro at Junior Nationals was still in sight. So I restarted the training process and you couldn't tell me anything after winning my first show. I thought I was hot shit and a ready-to-go pro.

Well, in June 2014, I traveled to Chicago as a green competitor who was unprepared for what Junior Nationals would bring. Men from coast to coast were in attendance and a lot of them were monsters compared to the contestants I'd seen in Cleveland a few months prior. I was in Class B again, according to my height. I felt good during the pump-up, but when I went on stage, I was definitely out-classed. I knew it as soon as those overhead lights hit. This wasn't Lakewood high school *at all*.

I was in the last call out and I didn't even place. Needless to say, I was heartbroken because I thought I'd found something I was good at after all those dark days in the hospital. All of my hopes and dreams were shattered at that moment. I couldn't hide my disappointment and I began to wonder if I'd been wasting my time. But, as always, Iisha came in clutch.

"So you're going to stop competing because it wasn't what you expected for your first time stepping on a national stage? What have we always instilled in our boys? We never lose; we either win or we learn," Iisha said.

So, with her words ringing in my head, I picked myself up and I got back on my grind. I'd fallen in love with the sport of bodybuilding as much as I'd loved track. Even with training partners and coaches on your team, it all boils down to how much work, dedication, and discipline you put into the process. So I began mapping out my strategy for the following year. Shortly afterward, I got a message from an Instagram follower named Gary C., who I'd competed against in Cleveland. He informed me that he was a coach and thought I had a lot of potential to be great at bodybuilding. Of course, my ego at the time was like, *Coach? Did you not see what I did on my own? Psssh, I don't need no coach.*

I still agreed to meet with Gary to hear his tips on posing since I was still new to it. He definitely knew what he was talking about and offered plenty of good advice, but my ego was also in the room. It convinced me not to listen to him and that ended up biting me in the ass.

NINE

I decided to continue to pursue competitive bodybuilding and entered another competition in Cleveland for another shot at a title. Unfortunately, I placed second. I was disappointed and regretful because I knew my loss was likely due to blowing off Gary's advice.

I continued training in preparation of returning to Chicago. I knew I needed to make much-needed progress on how I'd placed the previous year. Once I arrived, I earned another non-placement and returned home with a defeated spirit. How could I fight so hard to come back from all of my obstacles and challenges only to fail at the one achievement I was focused on chasing? Later that summer, I realized I had to swallow my pride and ditch my ego. This meant asking Gary for help. I'm glad I finally decided to do this because our friendship changed me for the better.

When Gary and I sat down to lay out the plan, I told him I had one dream: to compete in the Arnold. Although he tried to talk me out of it, due to his prior experience, I knew he was all in as my prep coach. We prepped for The Arnold Classic for 15 weeks. I sacrificed my time and stuck to a strict diet throughout Christmas and on my birthday in order to compete in this show. I'd grown up on action movies and Arnold Schwarzenegger is the epitome of bodybuilding to me.

When March 4, 2016 arrived, I traveled to the Columbus Convention Center. People attended the event from all over the world, speaking different languages while sharing a universal language and love of bodybuilding. Gary had shown me how to pose, which was the one skill I'd lacked while competing the previous two years. So I was feeling optimistic that I'd actually have a shot this time at placing. Unfortunately, on the morning of the show, we got hit with a monkey wrench. The officials decided to add quarter turns as a pose requirement an hour before the show began. Gary and I had never worked on them because it's more common in international competitions. Needless to say, I freaked out. After all the work we'd done leading up to that moment, I had yet another obstacle lying in my path.

We had no choice but to cram in a posing session utilizing quarter turns and Gary prepared me as quickly as he could. As I walked onto the stage for The Arnold, I felt alive again. Over the past several months, Gary had shown me that failure could be fueled in order to help me develop into a better athlete, competitor, and person overall. But none of those things could have prepared me for what I was in store for at The Arnold.

It was a fail. I realized the top ten wasn't in the cards for me that day. Had it not been for Gary, the defeat would have felt like the ones before at Chicago and at the hospital all over again. Yet, I took that L and began planning for my next show instead. My plan was to compete in the North American competition rather than Junior Nationals to obtain my pro card.

In May, a couple of months later, I decided to compete in the Mike Francis show in Pickerington, Ohio. The plan was to help me gain confidence after The Arnold and to establish a game plan to achieve pro status later that year. The goal of becoming a pro had consumed me, but it also gave me purpose. Having a family and career was great, but I needed that particular challenge to prove to myself that I was more than the label those doctors at Walter Reed had given me. I had a passion to help show the world that soldiers can bounce back and live fulfilling lives. I yearned to find peace for myself after what I'd missed over all these years.

That's how deep becoming an IFBB pro was for me in 2016. That grit and determination helped me crush the Mike Francis' show and I walked away with a first-place trophy!

TV Show Debut

My road to the pro card took a brief pause when I was selected to compete in a TV game show called the Power Triumph Games that aired on CBS Sports. Ten world-class military veteran athletes, who overcame catastrophic injuries, competed in a series of ten events for a $50,000 grand prize. Once again, I dreamed of moments like this while in the hospital. I saw it as a lifetime opportunity to be on national TV with my brothers and sisters in arms while showing the world how awesome we were, despite our perceived limits. When it was all said and done, I finished 4th. When I initially signed up for the show, water events weren't a part of it, but three weeks before filming, the producers threw a curveball and added one. As a child, I'd never learned to swim and the world was about to witness how bad I was at it on CBS Sports.

The water event required each athlete to memorize a puzzle while standing on a high board platform, then jump into 18 feet of water, swim to the other side and assemble the puzzle while 8 feet underwater. Because I'd won the first event, I was the first one to attempt the swimming event. Even though I knew damn well that I couldn't swim, their rescue divers were on deck, so I refused to back down from the challenge. Just like my time in the hospital, the moment I returned to the track, and the time I'd spent pushing myself to train in men's physique, the pool event was only a temporary challenge for me. They were no different than all of the previous ones and I couldn't risk losing a competition just because I wasn't good at every event. So, I took that dive off the two-story board and plummeted down in the water. I quickly resurfaced but immediately began yelling out, "HELP!"

Tim Kennedy, the show's co-host jumped in and retrieved me from the water. I gained the respect of my fellow competitors after that event. They all knew I couldn't swim and, just like our military service, I offered a brave face to the impending water no differently than I would on a battlefield. Landing in last place in that event had me climbing out of a hole for the rest of the competition and I was only able to finish in 4th place.

After a week of filming, it was time to head back home and get my bodybuilding training back underway. The North American competitions were only two and half months away and I needed to prepare. I was also finishing up my son's track season and would be starting a new school year soon. It's safe to say that my plate was beyond full. Gary had laid out one of our best plans for the year and I pushed myself to the max while training each day. I continued to train, even while in Texas for eleven days for my son's AAU Junior

Nationals track meet. I brought my own clean food and made the best use of the hotel gym. Thankfully, with my family's support, I maintained a disciplined routine toward my goal of obtaining my IFBB Pro card.

As I prepared to hit the stage a week before the show, Gary threw another curveball at me. He planned to hit the stage with me. We hadn't competed together since two years prior and I was excited to get up on stage with one of the sickest posers in the game, well in my opinion. As we approached the big day, and I had just purchased a new pair of board shorts, Gary gave me the best advice ever.

He said, "Believe in yourself as I believe in you, I want you to write inside of your shorts on the tag, 'I will go pro in these'." That inspirational quote, along with his belief in me let me know this was my year.

When I went to check-in at the Pittsburgh hotel, I learned I'd been placed in Class A and Gary was in Class B. We went through our last run-through of posing, and I got my famous cheat meal of a bacon cheeseburger and fries before game time the next morning.

The next morning, I woke up early and threw on some music. God must have wanted to get through to me because the first song on Pandora was, once again, Kanye's "Champion". I felt a distinct calm fall over me. I drove to the venue and patiently waited for my time. Having Gary with me made it easier to control my anxiety. In fact, I felt confident because the routine we'd put together was one of a kind.

Finally, I heard them announce, *men's physique lineup*. I knew it was game time. I had my final talk with God before walking onto the stage. I thanked Him for a second chance at life and for allowing me to find peace. I thanked Him that the past 5 years had only made me stronger. Even when I'd lost faith for a spell, He stayed by my side and continued to walk on this journey with me. I made a promise to keep living in my purpose and to always keep Him first, no matter how dark my days may get.

I walked on that stage and performed my routine. Gary felt that the world needed to know who I was and why those injuries existed because my story was bigger than I knew. He added nothing more than a simple military salute at the end. You would have thought the thunderous applause I got that day was just based on that. When we lined back up and they started call-outs, my jaw almost hit the ground when my number was called. All I could hear was Gary behind the curtain going nuts while still trying to get ready for his class, which was up next.

This man had focused on coaching me the whole time instead of focusing on himself. His main goal was to ensure that I held down my spot, split in the middle with another competitor. Finally, they let the top five walk off the stage and I'd finally achieved first call outs at a national-level show. The only thing left to do was wait for finals that night to see how things would shake out. Gary was cool as a cucumber because he already knew my outcome. Although he wasn't as successful with his class, he never wavered in his support for me. He was serious about being the best coach he could be for me.

As finals began, I was anxious and excited to see how I'd placed. Regardless of the results that year, it was still going to be my best year. Arnold hadn't been the best start for me, but I'd bounced back with Mike Francis. To earn a top-five finish at North Americans on top of that let me know that I wasn't doing too bad.

We lined back up on stage for the top five awards. They announced the fifth-place finisher through the third-place finisher and I was still standing. I knew that no matter how I finished, I had finally made my dream and goal come true that night. From that point on, I would be recognized as an IFBB Pro.

I was called out second behind a very great competitor who actually went on to win the overall title as well. So, I considered it to be a phenomenal second-place finish. As I smiled, I shed tears of gratitude because I'd accomplished something that, five years ago, no one could have predicted. I was the first-ever partial amputee in National Physique Committee (NPC) history to earn a men's physique IFBB Pro card. There are multiple service members that compete, but I've become one of a kind. Had it not been for the unconditional love and support of my family, friends, and Gary, who knows how much longer I would have struggled trying to figure things out on my own.

My journey from Iraq, through being hospitalized and returning home has been nothing short of ups and downs. We are given multiple choices in life and different ways to approach them. How we approach those choices leads us on different paths to uncovering our purpose in life. No matter the path we take or the details of the journey, we will fulfill our purpose if we stay focused on what's important.

Although I briefly lost my way, God has returned me to my path and my purpose in life. My struggles have since become my success and my injuries have fueled my drive. I was a husband, a father, a veteran, a teacher, and now I'm an IFBB Pro, living my life peacefully and fueled by strength and guidance from God. Although

I encountered more than my share of physical, emotional, and mental struggles, in the end, I didn't allow my temporary circumstances to dictate the endless possibilities of my future. Now, I'm blessed with a mind and spirit that are free from the horrors that once threatened to overtake me.

Yeah, they were definitely wrong to count this one out.

ACKNOWLEDGMENTS

I want to take this time to acknowledge some very special people in my life, because of you I'm here and this is all possible. Thank you to my literary team. To my developmental editor, Eryka Parker, thank you for helping me tell this story in the way it deserved to be told. I'd also like to thank my brother and cover designer, Miguel Hernandez for his dedication to this project.

I thank my Lord Savior Jesus Christ for giving me a second chance at life. I know all things are possible because of Him.

I want to thank my wife Iisha Collier. This woman has been my rock over these years. Through her drive and constant love I was able to accomplish more than anyone believed I could. She gives me strength even to this day, and because of that I will always honor her and love her.

Next, I want to thank my children (Malachi, Corwyn, and Aaron). You boys are my why. I never wanted you all to see me at my lowest, but you did, and you always encouraged me to keep going. It's because of you that I've continued to push myself so I could be the example of what it means to be a man, father, and husband.

I want to thank my father, Felton Collier. No matter what you have always sacrificed and put your children first. You gave up vacation days, sleep, and other countless hours just to ensure I was good. I can never repay you for everything, but I promise to keep making you proud.

Next, I want to thank my mother, Vickie Collier. Although our relationship is unique, you came back into my life and filled it with so much joy. I'm glad to have spent the second half of my life with you and building a new bond. Thank you for the countless conversations and love over these last few years.

Lastly, I want to dedicate this to my brother and sister, Felton and Victoria. When it comes to siblings and having each other's back, you two have always been there. I thank you both for being there during one of the most difficult times in my life and continuing to be there. As the middle child you guys definitely made me tougher.

I also want to thank a host of family, friends, and loved ones who've supported me over the years.

ABOUT THE AUTHOR

Corwyn "CJ" Collier was born in Nashville, Tennessee and moved to Cleveland, Ohio at the age of 7. He joined the Army National Guard and completed one tour in Iraq as a military police officer. He was struck by a roadside bomb while on tour. He has since competed in men's physique and became the first wounded/partial amputee vet to earn his IFBB pro card. Corwyn has been featured in Men's Health Magazine, Bodybuilding. com, and Fitness magazine. He has also been featured on a television show called the Triumph Games and in the Hulu documentary, Alive.

Corwyn is a high school teacher and head track coach. He lives with his wife and three sons in Northeast Ohio.

Made in the USA
Columbia, SC
08 November 2021

48528248R00050